Facebook Marketing

A Comprehensive Guide for Building Authority, Creating Engagement and Making Money Through Facebook

Mark Smith

Table of Contents

Introduction

Congratulations on downloading your personal copy of *Facebook Marketing: A Comprehensive Guide for Building Authority, Creating Engagement and Making Money through Facebook.* Thank you for doing so.

The following chapters will discuss some of the basics that you need to know in order to get started with Facebook marketing. It is one of the best marketing options that you can use to really form a relationship with your customers and promote your business. This book is going to spend some time talking about how to get started and will offer tips, proven strategies, and wisdom nuggets for building a powerful and profitable Facebook business.

The techniques shared in this book will be as straightforward and actionable as possible so even beginners can get their feet wet in the lucrative world of Facebook marketing.

There are plenty of books on this subject on the market, thanks again for choosing this one! Every effort was made to ensure it is full of as much useful information as possible, please enjoy!

Chapter One: Introduction to Facebook Marketing

Did you know that about 1.09 billion internet users log in to Facebook daily, with the number growing at a staggering 16% each year? It is one of the most popular social media platforms that account for 77% of all social media logins. Little wonder, then, those millions of ambitious online entrepreneurs are tapping into this beehive of viral activity related to both-personal and business accounts.

According to a Quicksprout survey, 80% of social media users in the United States prefer connecting with brands via Facebook.

Facebook is a brilliant medium for engaging visitors, building authority, driving traffic to your website and increasing your credibility as a brand. It helps you laser target your audience, and convert these interested people into leads, ultimately creating a base of loyal customers. Thus any business can leverage the power of Facebook to boost engagement, optimize their presence and build a solid brand.

Yes, it can be challenging to master the nuances of social media as it's a dynamic platform that keeps adding, deleting and modifying features. However, once you progress through the learning curve, your business can benefit tremendously from the power of a buzzing Facebook page.

Think of it this way. You've recently met a woman/man you fancy, and would love to spend the rest of your life with them.

What would be your best approach? Befriend them. Get to know more about their likes and dislikes, while striking a meaningful friendship based on common goals and interests. You may ask them out for coffee initially, build a rapport, and then do long dinner-movie dates. Eventually, you may pop the question, and spend the rest of your life with the man/woman you really dig.

What do you think would've happened if you would have simply walked up to them on seeing them for the first time and popped the question? Chances are they would've thought you are nuts, and simply scooted in the opposite direction to never see you again in this lifetime. A perfectly wonderful chance ruined.

This pretty much sums up how the social media works too, and why it is such a brilliant platform for increasing your chances of success. It helps you build a rapport with potential customers through engagement and conversation. You can't simply launch a business and expect people to queue up for buying. Any astute business person will realize that the customers buy from brands and people they love. People have got to love you and your brand to be able to relate to it and buy from you. This can be super effectively accomplished through engagement, conversation and constant communication with potential customers.

Social media marketing isn't different from dating. You're wooing your customers through engagement, making your brand appealing, offering value to potential buyers, and finally turning them into lifelong buyers. Facebook helps you create a strong base of loyal customers who act as your brand evangelists. They help spread a good word about your products or services within their social circle.

Did you ever move countries or cities? What was it like? A bit of culture shock? Of course, it can be perplexing to a new language, diverse people, and a different culture. You need to know about the accepted norms to fit in or learn about local customs and behavior before you gain the complete trust of locals.

This is how Facebook or any social media platforms works too. There are spoken and unspoken rules of the game that you must learn to adhere to if you want to build a desirable brand and profitable business.

One of the biggest advantages of using Facebook for your business is that it's a highly versatile platform that can be channelized to achieve multiple business goals. Your business goals can be anything from increasing conversions to building authority to boosting engagement. With its multiple tools, resources, and functions, Facebook can you achieve virtually any business goal.

Think of it as an online counterpart of a water cooler or an erstwhile town square. People collect near a water cooler (or town square in earlier times) and discuss just anything they fancy that brings them together. They share jaw dropping details about the latest breaking news or Game of Thrones episode while forging strong connections over shared conversation. It gets so interesting that they actually look forward to the next informal, engaging meeting at the designated spot.

If you've attended a cocktail party where you barely know anyone, you're doing pretty much a live version of what social media or Facebook marketing entails. You try to spot people who might be interested in you or who you share common interests with. There is a preliminary introduction where you get to know people. You crack jokes, build a connection by engaging others, have a meaningful conversation, and eventually promised to stay in touch with people. If you are interesting and authoritative, people will remember you (brand building) and look forward to meeting you again.

Facebook is an online cocktail party, where brands and customers are getting to know, and benefitting each other. When you post interesting and valuable stuff that your audience appreciates, people like your brand. They find it familiar and appealing, and establish a connection, which eventually helps when it comes to making a purchasing decision. Facebook is not merely a platform for selling (though it serves this purpose well too), it is also a powerful resource for building relationships.

Let's take two newly launched brands of soaps. Soap A barely has a social media or Facebook presence. They channelize all their resources print and billboard ads, hoping to make their brand familiar and desirable among their target audience.

Soap B, on the other hand, has a powerful Facebook presence. It posts thoroughly researched, easy to share, interesting and valuable information related to hygiene, skin care, and beauty.

Their target audience loves to share the posts the Brand B because it makes them look really smart and well-informed within their social circle. The brand's page is abuzz with activity, with people sharing lots of information. If people are given a choice between

Brand A and Brand B on a supermarket shelf, which brand do you think they are likelier to pick? Brand B will have a more engaged audience, which may make its recall and recognition value higher. People can relate to Brand B on a more personal level because it has made an effort to establish personal connections with its target audience. This is the true power of social media, which can be used to grow a variety of businesses.

You'll learn some of the best Facebook marketing strategies right here, which have the potential to skyrocket your business. Hop aboard, and get ready for the adventure of a lifetime!

Chapter Two: Facebook Marketing Tips for Beginners

Here are some highly proven and effective Facebook marketing tips to keep you ahead in the learning curve if you are just getting started with the seemingly big bag world of social media marketing.

1. Build a Business Profile

It's astounding how many people make this faux pas and lose out in the bargain. As a basic thumb rule, never ever do business through a personal profile. Build a distinct business profile page that effectively represents a brand. These pages don't appear too different from personal profiles but have a series of tools through which your audience can endorse your brand by liking the page, viewing regular updates, and commenting on your posts.

Creating a distinct brand page maximizes your business's chances of reaching out to a large number of interested customers. Also, it is against Facebook's Service Terms and Conditions to use personal profiles for anything other than personal interactions.

Also, if you've created a personal profile page for your brand or business, you should consider converting it into a business page. This way you'll still retain your personal account, while simultaneously having a business page.

Keep in mind that a profile can be converted into a business page just once. Once you've converted the personal account into a business, Facebook transfers your profile picture along with the cover picture to the new page. The page's name on the personal account becomes its business page name. Facebook offers tons of features that help move information from the personal profile page to a business page (takes 14 days from the date of conversion).

Choose friends from your personal profile to like your page automatically; however, posts on your personal profile will not be transferred to the new business page. The business page can also be managed via your personal account.

to convert your personal account into a Facebook business page:

1. Click on
    https://www.facebook.com/pages/create/migrate

2. Next, go to the "Get Started" button and follow all instructions to successfully migrate a personal business profile into a proper Facebook business page.

Having a business page offers me you multiple advantages, including the opportunity to laser target customers through Facebook's paid promotion feature and the ability to create events.

2. Create an Appealing and Memorable Vanity URL

Yes, the social media is as much about visual brilliance as it's about content and substance. Vain as it sounds, your page has to look gorgeous to pique the curiosity of people enough to come and explore it.

Once you've built a business page, Facebook assigns a random number to the URL, which means your page looks something like

facebook.com/pages/businessname/2346578.

A pro tip if you want to increase your page's shareable value or make it easy to find is to create a more identifiable, appealing, and memorable URL such as

Facebook.com/Sunshineflorists.

Go to General Account Settings, and change your URL into a more recognizable page name from the Username option.

3. Add a Recognizable and Attention Grabbing Cover Photo

Next, add a stunning cover photo to create a desirable visual effect. Facebook allows 851 x 315-pixel cover images right at the top of your business page. Optimize your cover photo to grab the attention of your target audience, hook them enough to explore more about your products/services, and offer an efficient mobile browsing experience.

Your cover photo is the first thing people spot when they visit your page because it occupies considerable space, and strategically sits right at the top of the page. Here are some tips to keep in mind to optimize the appeal for your Facebook cover photo.

1. This seems like a given, but it's still not funny how many people actually overlook it. Follow Facebook's guidelines when it comes to creating a cover photo because it's just not the smartest thing to lose your page for a cover photo guideline violation.

Read the full terms and conditions before you go about uploading a cover photo for the business page. In general keep in mind that your cover image is public. Don't make it misleading, irrelevant or deceptive. Also, don't infringe someone else's copyright simply by lifting images from various sources.

2. Ensure that the image is optimized to the right size and resolution. It should be 828 x 315 px on a desktop interface, and 640 x 360 px tall on a mobile interface. Make sure you get these dimensions right while designing the photo, otherwise you'll keep tweaking it while uploading the image. Design anything smaller than this, and Facebook will end up stretching the image, making it look unprofessional and tacky. To make your task easier, you can simply download a pre-sized Facebook cover photo template with a simple Google search.

3. The placement of profile pictures on Facebook makes it tough to view a section of the cover photo unless it's clicked on. In addition to the profile picture, the page name and buttons also hide a section of the cover photo. Keep this in mind and don't include important pieces of imagery or content in these portions, which aren't immediately visible or viewable to users.

    Since Facebook positions your profile picture on the left, it is a good strategy to right align your cover photograph to maintain a balance, and make your brand/product clearly visible, while also appearing more aesthetically elegant. You will be able to attract greater focus to the brand or product by right aligning your Facebook cover image.

Ensure the photo is visible for mobile viewing since more than half of your user base will view your page from handheld devices. Compared to the desktop, a larger portion of your cover page is hidden by the profile picture. The page name also appears on the cover photo, which impacts its visibility. Keep all this in mind before designing your cover photo.

4. Try incorporating your Facebook cover photo with other design elements on the page to maintain consistency and uniformity in your brand's visual identity. If the dominant colors in your logo are red and yellow, stick a cover photo where red and yellow are prominently displayed. Don't see it as an isolated or individual design element. Rather make the cover photo a part of a larger overall canvas that balances multiple design elements to draw optimal attention on your Facebook page.

Some of the best business pages combine their cover photo and profile picture and make it look integrated, like two sections of a single brand canvas. This is a subtle, yet compelling way to conveying your brand identity.

4. Add an Awesome Profile Picture

Facebook allows you to upload a recognizable profile picture such as a company logo image of your products/services or a headshot if you are a solo entrepreneur. If you want your target audience to find and like your page, choose your profile image smartly. Keep in mind that it is also displayed as a thumbnail image next to every update.

The dimensions of a Facebook profile photo are 180 x 180 px (160 x 160 px on desktop machines).

5. Optimize The About Section

When people need more information about your brand/business, they are most likely to browse through the "About" section of your page.

Ensure the page is optimized for social media and search engines by including a detailed and impactful description of your business using the most relevant keywords that define the enterprise/brand. Give visitors a good feel of what the page is about in the opening lines of your description. A brief section of the detailed "About" description will be extracted and displayed under "Short Description by Facebook.

Include as many details as possible that visitors may find useful in your "About" section, including a phone number, physical address (if required), website URL, email, business opening hours, price range, a link to your product and service catalog and other relevant information.

6. Earn The Very Responsive Badge

One of the first things you must aim to accomplish after creating a business page is earning a "very responsive to messages" Facebook awards pages who have a response percentage of 90% and a response time of less than 15 minutes over a period of one week.

Having this badge makes customers view you as a prompt, communicative and reliable business which makes an effort to connect with customers. It shows you are tuned into your audience's queries and care enough to offer them a speedy response. Even if you can't give an immediate solution to the customer, try and keep your response time high by replying and letting them know that you will get back to them with a solution as soon as you've figured it out. It makes you come across as professional, friendly and concerned.

7. Include Milestones

Use the "Milestones" feature on Facebook to highlight your brand's most notable achievements. Events you can include under the milestone feature are the year your brand/business was launched, awards it won in the past, product releases and other noteworthy accolades.

Users will find your brand more credible and authoritative when you display your accomplishments. Basically, a great way to blow your own trumpet and keep customers in the loop about your brand's evolution.

8. Call to Action

Facebook has included in what is being hailed as one its best business page features. It allows visitors to place easy, visible, and effective call to action buttons on their page. Select from one of the pre-defined call to action buttons such as "contact us", "book now", "sign up", "use app" and more. This is a great tool for linking the relevant website page or landing page with your Facebook business page.

How to Add a CTA button to Your Facebook Business Page

Log in and go to your Facebook Business page.

Click on the "Call to Action" button positioned on top of the page next to the Like button.

It's no rocket science really. Make it easy for your customers to do what you want them to do by telling them what they're supposed to do.

9. Create Unique Page Tabs

Facebook offers a set of predefined page tabs such as About, Photos, Likes and other similar options. However, you can also create custom tabs that can perform functions similar to landing pages within the business page. The tabs are located at the top of your business page. For example, if you want to invite entries for a draw or competition, create a custom "enter competition" or "submit your entry" tab for the purpose. Link it to the submit entries page on your website.

How to Create Unique Page Tabs?

Sign in to your business page. Select the "More" tab.

Next, select the Manage Tabs option from a dropdown list.

10. Post Best Blog Content

Most businesses rely on social media to offer their target audience a steady stream of valuable and interesting content. Avoid populating the timeline with every blog post. Cherry pick only the best ones that are entertaining, useful, relevant and informative.

Several blogging platforms offer a feature where the software automatically updates each new blog postand publishes it on your page. All you need to do this sync your blog page with your Facebook business page, and auto-publish content. However, it's best to publish content that will engage interested fans, and keep them hooked.

Also, each time you post a blog link on Facebook, the page pulls a short description along with an image. This description is extracted from your blog page's meta description (the description that is specifically created to show up as the page's description on the search engine results page preview). Ensure your meta description is relevant, accurate and well-written.

without a properly written meta description, Facebook will simply pull out anything it finds without the relevant keywords and phrases, which is a huge lost opportunity. It will hamper the overall user experience, and fail to attract customers to your business.

Sum up your posts in under 155 characters by drafting a power-packed meta description. Don't waste your valuable space real estate in including preposterously long links to the post within the post. The thumbnail URL is enough to send readers to your blog post. Use your space wisely for piquing the reader's curiosity or grabbing their attention.

Many newbie marketers misleadingly believe that posting frequently increases the visibility of their posts. Facebook's algorithms aren't as straightforward. It all boils down to the quality of posts, and the engagement it attracts. Posting more frequently won't help you reach more people unless you are targeting people in different time zones and have a clear objective for posting frequently.

Poor quality posts that receive little response end up affecting your statistics, and can even go on to reduce your visibility among your followers. Facebook has slick practices in place to filter out low-quality and irrelevant posts. Put up top quality posts only, and watch your numbers soar.

Give importance to quality over quantity by being selective about your posts. Don't overwhelm your target audience by drafting multiple posts. Rather, take the time to create delightful posts that your audience will love to share within their social circle.

Adorn your posts with high-quality visuals and videos to increase their appeal. Facebook posts with interesting and relevant visuals witness 2.3x greater engagement than imageless posts.

Even if you have a blog with several posts, optimize it for Facebook by adding new videos and slick images. Any fool-proof social media or Facebook strategy includes images, videos, infographics, tables, charts and screenshots that offer tremendous value to your audience.

Follow the 80-20 social media thumb rule, where 80 percent of your posts are dedicated to non-promotional posts (aimed at increasing engagement and establishing connections), while 20 percent posts are channelized towards directly promoting your products or services.

People don't really fancy being sold to on social media. They view it more as a platform for discussion, communication and forging connections. Therefore, your social media strategy needs to be subtle and more directed towards building a brand and making connections, which eventually turn into loyal customers.

11. Focus On Offering Value

As any internet or social media marketer will tell you, you must give value first to receive business from your customers later. Initially, the focus is only on building connections, credibility, and authority. Don't focus on hard selling in the early stages of your business.

For instance, if you run an organic products e-store, the standard marketing strategy would be to post images of your products and urge customers to buy them. However, this isn't how Facebook or social media marketing works.

Instead of hard selling your products, create blog posts about healthy, organic recipes using ingredients you sell. Share links of the recipes on your page. At the bottom of these recipes, subtly mention that these products can be easily sourced from your website.

In the above example, ensure your content strategy includes a variety of recipes catering to conscious eaters or health buffs such as "20 Easy to Make and Healthy Lunch Box Recipes For Kids" or "Simple and Healthy Smoothies for Diabetics" or "15 Healthy and Delicious One Pot Organic Meals." Do you get the drift?

Oreo's Facebook page is crazy popular because they connect with their fans by offering them tons of delicious, innovative and fun Oreo recipes, complemented by tempting images. They also use a bunch of clever and appealing hashtags. Who can resist?

Social media users lap up content that has high utility or informational value. They also love to share content that makes them look really smart among their friends. Post high-value, intelligently written and useful content, and people will be more than happy to spread the word.

Dove is another brand that has its social media strategy brilliantly figured out. They created a video a couple of years back, which earned them thousands of likes and about half a million views. The brand was barely mentioned in the video. Dove was simply focused on telling stories that evoke emotions and make their relatable.

They told stories about everyday women and encouraged their fans to tag women who inspired them, thus helping the brand get its word out without aggressively marketing their products. Women found these stories relatable and connected with the brand on an emotional, nostalgic level.

12. Images

Did you know that Facebook posts with images receive 84 percent higher link clicks than those with visuals? It's simple. Present people with stuff that looks stunning, is easy to understand and evokes some emotion.

Tell stories through pictures. It's called humanizing your brand. People love behind the scenes stories about businesses and brands. They like to think that they are dealing with real people who care about them and not factory bots.

Create everyday slice of life or behind the scenes posts about your business. Introduce your customers to your employees. Give them a peek about how the products they use are actually created.

Pictures of real people help people connect with your brand. While using images for Facebook posts, focus on people's faces. Facial profile images work well for Facebook posts.

Rather than using images of the product, include lifestyle images. You need to tap into your audience's aspirations by showing them the lifestyle your product/service represents. Use images that induce a strong sense of nostalgia. Make image galleries and collages if you want to share multiple images to make it easy for your audience to access all images in a single postrather than creating multiple, confusing posts.

Use bright, high resolution and eye-catching images. Low-lit images with dull colors don't receive much traction on the social media.

Well, people may say they are annoyed with constantly seeing pictures of where their friends are dining or what they are up to. However, the fact is, they are still viewing it. According to

Social Media Examiner, images make up for 87 percent of the content shared on Facebook.

Just browse through a few business pages, and you'll discover how a majority of them use stock photos rather than original images. Use real, natural photographs rather than generic stock images. Posts that have original, real pictures come across as more relatable and organic.

Another smart tip is to integrate your Instagram images in your Facebook feed.

Tap on the settings option in your Instagram account, and link your Facebook account. Every Time you take a picture, tap on the Facebook icon for sharing those pictures on your Facebook news feed.

13. Make Content Easy to Share

It is a golden nugget of wisdom in internet marketing circles that if you make anything too complicated for your audience, they are less likely to do it. This explains all the spoon-feeding (click here, visit our page, buy now etc. links).

People generally have less time and a shorter attention span when they are browsing the internet. They won't spend time trying to figure out things if it looks complicated or if they don't know what action to take.

Make sharing your posts a cakewalk for them by using prominent "Share" or "Like" buttons on your blog page. Use the Facebook Follow button to increase your reach. People can like your page with a single click, while also viewing the total number of likes received by the page. This sort of validates your page or offers social proof to prospective and existing customers.

Adding Facebook social share buttons encourages your web audience to connect and communicate with your brand on Facebook, while also increasing the reach of your content by sharing it.

with the Facebook Like Box, visitors can view your follower count and check recently posted content.

14. Schedule Posts in Advance

One of the most efficient ways to run a Facebook business page is to schedule your posts in advance either weekly or monthly. There are lots of last minute things which come upand can distract us away from a fixed schedule. This may pose a challenge to the pursuit of posting a steady stream of relevant and interesting content designed to engage your target audience.

Once you've identified the best time to post on Facebook, use applications such as HubSpot, Buffer or Hootsuite to schedule your posts for a particular date and time weekly or monthly. You can create an editorial calendar for the entire month. Consider festivals, holidays, and events etc. for the month while planning "hot" or viral posts in advance. The posts can be planned at the same time in advance every week for the entire week.

However, having said that, maintain a balance between pre-scheduled and timely posts to avoid turning your page into an automated machine where it loses a human touch. Ensure you're creating some real time posts too for engaging with fans or striking up a conversation to get their views on a recent development.

How to schedule posts in advance?

Start creating a post as you normally would.

Click on the down arrow sign located adjacent to Publish, and tap on Schedule.

Just below publication, choose the date and time when you wish to publish the post.

Select Schedule

You can also delete or make changes to scheduled posts.

Click edit to make changes to your post or select the down arrow icon to reschedule or delete the post.

Chapter Three: 13 Fantastic Tips for Boosting Engagement

It is little wonder that Facebook is among the most dominant content marketing platforms. The social networking site has a ton of fresh, dynamic and resourceful features that can be brilliantly integrated into your overall promotional strategy. Yes, we all know by now that it can be used to increase engagement, boost authority and build brands. Your half a million fans will be of little consequence if they aren't doing much on the page.

Have you ever thought about why some posts go viral, while others become ghost towns? Nope, it has got little to do with luck, and more to do with the timing of your post, the words you use and what is posted.

Facebook users react well to posts related to technology, travel/lifestyle, health, positivity and sports/games. A quick pro tip – if you include words such as "why", "how" or "most" on your posts, you are likely to garner higher likes, comments, and shares.

The million-dollar question is – how can you boost engagement through Facebook posts?

Here are 12 fantastic and proven tips to help boost your audience engagement.

1. Host Contests

This is one of the best strategies for improving engagement on your Facebook business page. It's such a no-brainer, yet marketers fail to channelize it effectively. The thrill of winning something gets people to take action, which can be used to your advantage. Use rewards, prizes, and freebies as an incentive to create a buzz about your brand.

One of the biggest advantages for marketers is that for a comparatively low-cost, you'll end up gaining plenty of exposure and brand awareness. If done right, it can be a brilliant payoff.

How to Create a Facebook Contest

1. Pick the Right Prize

The prize is what's going to make or ensure a successful run for your contest. Keep it relevant and appropriate to your business. A pro tip is to offer your audience gift cards for your business, which gives them a chance to get interested in or try your products/services.

Offering customers free iPads and iPhones will have them liking iPads and iPhones, not really your products or services. They may simply like your page or share your post for the sake of winning an iPhone without really being interested in your products or services.

However, if you are offering gift cards or freebies related to your products or services, you will get a bunch of targeted, interested customers who are interested in trying your products. For instance, if you sell baby care products and offer gift vouchers for the same, you'll get a ton of interested parents who are keen on trying your products liking your page or sharing your posts.

Giving prizes that are not relevant to your products or services won't really help boost conversions. However, a bunch of targeted consumers trying your products can help spread the word about them, especially in the initial stages of the business. You can include discounts or freebies on future purchases in the gift card too for encouraging customers to buy from you.

2. Make it Easy to Enter

Your aim is to increase the number of followers/fans and boost engagement for your business page. Make entering the contest easy for people to gain maximum response. You can ask social media users to like your page, share the contest post and tag friends who you think will be interested in the contest to be eligible for the contest/draw. Pick a winner by conducting a live draw.

Another popular way to get people to participate in contests is by focusing on user generated content. This is also a smart strategy for populating your business page with interesting content posted by users themselves. Ask customers to enter the draw by posting images, videos or slogans to enter. Create a hashtag, and let views use the hashtag while posting content on your business page. The audience can then vote for their favorite entry.

Include brief information about how to enter the contest on your post, and link to an outside web page for details about rules and regulations to avoid cluttering the Facebook contest post.

3. Attention Grabbing Title

A short, catchy call-to-action title helps maximize your contest response. For instance, "Enter to Win a $60 Gift Card For Our

Fabulous Range of Handmade Soaps." It's simple, descriptive and appealing. It tells visitors what they are supposed to do and the prize that awaits them in a straightforward manner.

You can also create a contest entry landing page, and ask them to enter their contact details. This will help you create an email list of people who may be interested in learning more about your products or services in future. Send people on email list updates, seasonal offers, and informative newsletters to keep them hooked.

4. Image

Use large, high-quality images to entice people into entering the contest. If you are giving away gift cards, use a large image of the gift card with its worth mentioned prominently on the image. Also, include images of products that were purchased for the given gift card amount.

2. Post Response Generating Posts

Pose an attention-grabbing yet simple question for drawing your fans into a conversation. For instance, if you run a travel/lifestyle/leisure related brand, posting images related to beaches or mountains with a simple caption like, "Hit Like if you want to spend a relaxed day on this tropical island" or "Hit like if you feel like grabbing an ice-cream Sundae Right Now." Simple yes/no type of questions can also help generate quick Facebook post traction.

Telling people what you want them to do will increase your page engagement. Ask interesting open questions, such as, "If you could take off to any destination of your choice, where would it be? Or "What food items are on your current craving list?" Keep posts engaging and relevant to your page.

Which is your favorite luxury car?

You can never really have enough ---------

How many times do you let the phone ring before answering?

Questions like these spark stimulating conversations and unimaginably funny answers. Get creative with your questions to draw your fans into a conversation.

Create posts that get people involved. If you are stuck with a decision, create a poll to gather feedback from your target audience. It gives you quick insights about exactly what your customers are looking for, along with boosting page engagement. Encourage fans to post testimonials of your products or services along with images.

If there's a raging topical issue or controversy related to your field, ask customers to share their views about the same. Keep the debate sane and healthy by establishing clear guidelines at the outset.

Urge people to share memories, moments and experiences or go slightly edgy with a controversial question. Ask direct questions or encourage people to share their favorite tips related to your products/services.

Make people feel wonderful about them by encouraging them to share innovative ideas about the different ways through which they use your products. You bet people love it when the spotlight's on them or when they are at the center of the conversation.

I simply love asking my page fans to pick between two choices. Pick a favorite between "A" or "B" or choose between "X" or "Y." This can create a lovely division between fans (evil in a fun way yes), which sparks further debate and conversation in the comments. Using current controversies is alright as long as you don't venture into sensitive topics such as politics and religion.

Whether your post bags a single comment or multiple comments, attempt to respond to each of them individually. Facebook lets you like comments, which is a great way for you to acknowledge their response. Of course, it will be a challenge to reply to hundreds of comments. However, taking that extra effort will make you come across as a caring, customer-focused organization that values its fans/buyers.

3. Post Shareable Content

Videos and infographics are currently the hottest content formats on the social media. If you can create a single infographic or list for summarizing everything that people need to know about a topic, there's no stopping fans from sharing it. Checklists or cheat-sheets are amazing from a viral perspective.

If your business relates to travel gear, you can create a handy backpacker's checklist or if you are an internet marketer, a quick content creation or topic generation (or headline generation) cheat sheet can do the trick.

Make it a valuable proposition for your target audience by putting together information that is time-consuming to research in an easily digestible format. For instance, you can put together a handy guide for travelers visiting a particular destination by including all important information in a single infographic.

People don't have the time to research and jot down important pieces of information on a single source, which is why infographics are hugely popular. You can create an infographic using an app like Canva or hire someone to do it.

4. Engage with Other Businesses

There's no stopping you from engaging on other pages, especially when they there's a synergy of products/services or a shared audience. For instance, if a wedding jewelry related business has posted something about weddings, you can chime in with your 2 cents too if you are a florist, wedding photographer or wedding cakes business. You aren't directly competing with the brand or there's no conflict of interest.

However, be mindful of not spamming other business pages on the Facebook landscape with your promotional posts. Keep it subtle and engage in a naturally meaningful manner. Add well-researched, detailed and thought-provoking comments to establish authority. You'll expose your brand to a large number of targeted customers if it's a popular page.

Who doesn't benefit from a bit of cross promotion and synergy? Encourage other pages within your industry to comment/post on your pages too. If you can work out a fruitful mutual sharing agreement, both pages can boost their organic reach and enjoy exposure to a wider base of potential customers. You can also create guest posts for other blogs, which they can share on their business page to increase your authority, credibility and brand awareness.

Round-ups are another fantastic way to get experts to share your posts on their pages. Ask influencers in your field to share their best tips on the given topic. Make a post about these tips by tagging these influencers and getting them to share the round-up on their pages.

Everyone loves to be seen as an expert among their fans and audience, which means the influencers will most likely share these posts (which pitch them as an expert) on their news feed, thus giving your brand exposure among fans/followers of a bunch of experts or popular business pages.

If you find particularly interesting images on your fan's news feed, take permission to post it and give them credit for it.

Social media is based on a strong sharing economy, which means you mustn't shy away from posting relevant, valuable and useful content from other players in the niche.

One pro tip to get a lot of organic likes for your page is to enable the "Similar Page Suggestions" on your page. Go to "Settings" and enable the "Similar Page Suggestions" option. This way when people like pages that are similar to yours, Facebook automatically suggests your page to them. Not many people know about this feature but it can help you some great organic likes from interested folks.

5. Boost Posts

Facebook offers business page administrators/owners a paid boost post option to create more engagement on specific posts. You can either boost posts among existing followers and their friends (which means the post will be visible to a higher number of fans on their feed) or select a predefined audience (based on audience demographics, interests, hobbies, and pages they've liked) to boost your posts. These posts will show up on the news feed on the selected audience group, which means a higher engagement for your posts.

Boost your most popular blog posts that have witnessed a considerable swarm of traffic. Post it on your business page, and use the boost post option. There's no need to invest thousands of dollars on advertising. You can start with $25 by targeting folks who've already liked your page and people on their friends list. It may be enough to give your posts a slight nudge.

Though there's low chance of seeing thousands of likes or share, boosting posts can increase engagement and initiate conversation. It can get people to spark a conversation, while also making them aware of your products or services. This can increase your organic reach within their networks. Use this strategy for high-quality, information blogs where you are offering clear solutions to desperate problems faced by people. It works well for posts that answer the most compelling questions about a topic or offer people high-value takeaways.

How do you look for your blog's most popular content? Go to Google Analytics. Select Behavior, followed by Site Content and All Pages. Go through the metrics for every page to know your most popular posts.

How to boost posts on Facebook? Here's a handy step by guide to get you started.

Go to your business page

Select the post you wish to boost (remember to pick only high-quality posts which have proved their popularity on your web page or posts you think have the potential to be popular).

Select the "Boost Post" button located just above the post. If the button isn't activated, it will stay unclickable, which simply means that this particular post cannot be boosted. There can be several reasons for this including the like the business page may be unpublished or you may not have sufficient admin rights to boost a post or you may need to set up a payout method.

Go to the Audience field. Carefully pick the audience you would like to reach from the given options. There's also an option to "Create New Audience." You can start from scratch by targeting users based on their location age, interests, gender and behavior.

Next, click the dropdown to pick a budget for boosting your post. You can either select a predefined budget or opt for the "Choose Your Own" optionand enter an amount of your choice.

Pick a duration for which you want the post to be boosted. Enter the end date of the boosted post in the "Run this ad until" section.

Select a preferred payment method from the given options. If you haven't done any paid promotions on Facebook before, you'll have to add a payment method to your Facebook ads account.

Finally, click "Boost."

6. Stay Persistent

You won't believe how many people actually give up building strong business pages on Facebook when they would've been a roaring success simply by tweaking their strategy a bit. Don't expect overnight success. It's not like you build a page, and have people swarming to it with a million likes and thousands of shares. Many of your initial posts will barely have any engagement. Keep posting a variety of stuff to test what works best for your market.

If a particular type of post hasn't performed well, opt for another. See what other businesses in your domain are doing successfully and incorporate the same into your social media content strategy.

While social media marketers will also emphasize on posting relevant posts (including yours truly), it's alright to have fun occasionally. Experiment with a funny quote or laugh-worthy meme that your fans can relate to. Pose random questions.

Don't always keep the focus on your products or services. Help you fans have some fun! You may not get business through that funny meme but it makes you likable. It will set the tone for another post, which can include a link to your website.

People generally use Facebook to make connections and browse through informative and entertaining posts. Try different types of posts to measure ones that draw a maximum response from your target audience or stir them into interaction.

Facebook offers some of the best audience insights and analytics for your page. Spot patterns and trends, and reinvent for strategy according to these valuable insights. For example, if you see a huge surge in fans within the week, look closely at your recently posted content. Figure out a clear reason for these trends, and continue posting more of the same if it's working.

Where do I check my Facebook business page insights?

Log in to your Facebook account.

Click the page for which you want to view the statistics from the left sidebar.

Click "View Insights" on the right sidebar of your business page to check interaction statistics for the last month. The statistics will include insights such as number of new likes, post views and other user activity represented through figures and charts.

Social media is all about creating a run-up to the actual decision. You're setting the stage by establishing relationships, engaging your audience and making your brand desirable before you actually go for the kill. Remember the 80-20 rule?

10. Post at the Optimal Time

Posting at a time when your audience is most likely to be on Facebook increases the visibility and exposure of your message. This is a question most newbie marketers struggle with simply because there isn't a single time for all enterprises.

The best days and times to post on Facebook depends on the type of business.

For instance, if you are targeting home-makers, they are likely to be online at a different time (later mornings or afternoons) than working professionals (late evenings and weekends). It also depends on the type of post you are targeting, and the region the post is meant for.

There is, of course, some reliable data on the best times to post on Facebook, though you must research the social media browsing habits of your target audience to arrive at the best days and times unique to your business.

As a general guideline, the optimal time to post content on Facebook is 3.00 p.m. on Wednesdays. Other good days and times to post are 12:00 to 1:00 p.m. on weekends, and 1:00 to 4:00 p.m. on Fridays and Thursdays.

Engagement rates are known to be 18% higher towards the fag-end of the week (Thursday and Friday), and on other weekdays from 1:00 to 4:00 p.m. This is especially true for businesses related to leisure, travel, vacations, and hobbies. The click through rates are known to be higher at the above mentioned times. Also, since there is 10% increase in Facebook activity on Fridays (and people tend to be merrier at the prospect of the oncoming weekend), it is generally considered a good day for posting positive, funny and uplifting content.

The most unfavorable times to post on Facebook include after 8:00 p.m. and after 8:00 a.m. on weekends. Of course, use this as a general guideline and not rule of the book for posting on your business page.

You still need to investigate what are the best times for audience engagement based on trial and error. Try posting at different times during the first few days, and check when you can elicit the maximum response or engagement from your target audience.

If you are beginning from scratch and have no data of your own to gauge what the audience likes or dislikes, simply go to a platform like BuzzSumo.com. Do a search based on your niche or main keywords, and find a list of posts which have received maximum likes and shares on Facebook.

The platform offers tons of features, including the check which pages/posts are performing particularly well for a competitor. It is also a nice place to find influencers in your domain for some much-needed cross promotions.

11. Keep Posts Short

Don't convert your Facebook business page into a blog. Social media users are not on Facebook to read long-winded content. Keep it concise and engaging. Posts that are under 50 characters garner maximum engagement. Adding characters beyond that reduces your chances of engagement. Unless long posts have proven to work for your particular niche or audience, it is best to keep them below 50 characters.

Don't sound preachy or overly promotional; inspire people to connect with you by sharing stories visually.

Share images based on the core values related to your business. You'll be the ultimate social media magnet if you share the business/brand's passion with customers, creating an almost cult like following. Your business can be passionate about organic food (if you run a food related business). Build a community by infusing the same level of passion in your followers through short and interesting posts.

Share a sense of purpose that genuinely inspires people. In the above example, it can be about healthy eating, going organic or sticking to vegan meals. Find a clear sense of purpose and spread it to your fans. Post pictures of your brand connecting with real people to add the much-needed human touch. Share uplifting and inspiring quotes that trigger your fans into action.

List posts, infographics and "how to" articles that stir curiosity fare effectively on the Facebook platform. If you do a BuzzSumo search for "healthy eating", you'll discover that the top-performing posts are "18 Make Ahead Meals to Eat Healthy without Even Trying" and "How to Eat Healthy Whole Foods, Plant-Based Diet on $50 Per Week?" Well, everyone wants to know how one can eat healthy on a budget of $50/week. Spark a sense of curiosity, and you'll have them hooked.

12. Use the Power of Facebook Groups

Groups are an excellent platform for building a community based on shared interests. They bring together people sharing a common passion and can stir greater dialogue and engagement than regular business pages. Track down niche groups related to your industry or create your own group, and link it to your main business page.

Give it an easily searchable and relevant name. Include a brief and appropriate description for the group so people can find it easily. Keep posting content that inspires interaction about topics related to the group. Encourage group members to post their queries or start a discussion. You can even share your blog posts or business page posts within the group to give them greater exposure.

Building a loyal and engaged community is the foundation of launching a successful social media enterprise. Though maintaining a busy group can be time-consuming and tedious, it may offer brilliant pay offs in future.

Groups are incredible when it comes to building a network around your business. For instance, if you are a consultant for small and mid-sized businesses, you can build a group around "power entrepreneurs." Similarly, if you sell camping gear or organize camping holidays, start a "camping enthusiasts" group. Encourage people to share their blogs, inspiring pieces of content and topics that get everyone fired up into a discussion.

How to get the group rolling?

- Post questions. If you don't know what to talk about, simply ask people what they'd like to discuss.
- Host events such as an online webinar, Hangout session or in person events. Groups give you a fabulous opportunity to connect with like-minded folks in person.
- Encourage member introductions. Ask people to share a little bit of their background, passions and business interests. Create conversations and/or connections based on sharing details about people's aspirations, goals, and interests.
- Conduct polls about what people would like to hear about and discuss in the group.

13. Celebrate Holidays and Festivals

Fans love it when you add a bit of holiday/festival cheer to your posts. It gets them into a joyful and celebratory mode. Ensure to create posts for special events, and participate in the festive spirit. It reveals an interesting persona, while also demonstrating your sense of awareness about the latest happenings. This makes the business look more human and less robotic, which is really what social media marketing is about.

Find out if the holiday applies to a particular community or it's celebrated globally. Use it as an occasion to greet you fans and connect with them.

For instance, if it's International Women's Day, you can share an appreciation post about the company's women employees. Give a brief and interesting backdrop, and mention how they add value to the organization. Fans love inside details about people who run the show from behind the scenes.

People are generally in a more joyous, positive and spending mode during festivals, which means it may be easier to get them to make purchases in a promotional post, following a cheery festival wish post.

Chapter Four: Killing it with Facebook Advertising

It is no secret that Facebook offers one of the best paid advertising programs on the internet. The biggest advantage of opting for a paid promotion is that you can target your customers based on just about anything on their profile from the kind of movies they enjoy watching to life events (recently married or engaged) to their profession and interests. Wait, there's more – think birthdays, zip code, relationship status, and education.

This gives marketers looking to target a specific group a clear edge for promoting their products and services. Facebook is a goldmine for smart marketers who know how to use its comprehensive user database to their advantage.

Take for example, you own a gymnasium in Phoenix, and want to target health buffs that have moved to the city recently, you can target your ads only towards them. Similarly, if you sell golf kits online throughout the United States, you can target golf enthusiasts living in the country.

This saves you from throwing away precious advertising money by promoting your products/services to people who have scant interest in them. There's no denying that Facebook's ads can be super profitable if you know how to play with them effectively.

According to an eMarket survey, almost 96% of social media users consider Facebook advertising as the most result-generating paid promotion methods across multiple social media platforms.

A *New York Times* report states that on an average, users typically spend an hour on Facebook each day, which explains why Facebook advertising budgets are skyrocketing. You are leaving too much money on the table for competitors if you aren't leveraging the power of Facebook advertising.

You know why people hate YouTube ads? Because they interrupt a user's viewing experience. Facebook has tweaked their advertising feature to seamlessly and naturally integrate its paid promotions into a user's news feed without disrupting his experience. This is why viewers are less annoyed and more receptive to these ads.

So, what are the best tips to get started with Facebook advertising? I've got your back here too.

Here's a handy guide to help you advertise like a pro on Facebook.

1. To begin advertising on Facebook, go to your page's "Ads Manager" section.

2. Before you begin advertising, you must have a clear objective for the paid promotion.

What do you hope to achieve through the paid promotion? More page likes? More engagement on specific posts? Higher website conversions? App installations and other similar marketing goals.

Once you pick your advertising goal, Facebook will display the option that works best for accomplishing your marketing objective.

3. Pick your audience. In the beginning, you'll have to test various audience groups to identify the ones which produce optimal results. Based on the criteria specified by you, Facebook will present an Audience Definition tool to the right of the audience field option. It takes all you pre-defined properties to come up with a potential reach figure.

Facebook's audience targeting fields are so vast, it's virtually impossible to include them all here. You can target users based on their location, gender, languages, relationships, finances, ethnicity, life events, politics, interests, hobbies, connections, behavior and much more.

There is a Custom Audience option too where you target a set of predefined audience members in your organization's database or people who've visited your blog or used your application. This option allows you to target customers based on very specific criteria.

Once you've discovered an audience group that has responded well to your ads, you can save these audiences by clicking on saving the audience group for later (so you don't have to go through the process of picking the audience all over again).

Pro tip – While the campaign is running, if you gauge that a particular group is responding really well to the ad and bringing down your cost per like/click, you can edit your audience options instantly. For instance, say you are promoting an adventure travel page and learn that men are offering a lower cost per click for your page. You may want to edit your audience settings to men only.

4. Facebook offers you the option to select how and where you want your ads to appear. Advertisers have the option of picking desktop feed, mobile feed, and right column ads.

You can select the ones that are most beneficial for your business, but mobile feed ads perform much better than desktop feed ads or right column ads (least favorable). Most people access their social media accounts through handheld devices, which makes mobile feed ads effective.

5. Set a daily budget. If you want your ad to run on a daily budget, specify your daily limit in the Daily Budget option. For instance, if you enter $25 as your daily budget, Facebook will run an ad on a daily budget of $25 until you end the campaign.

If you want the campaign to run for a fixed number of days, enter the end date within the "Run Campaign Until" option. Your ad will only run until a specified date. When you're experimenting in the beginning, go with a modest budget.

6. Creating the ad. NNo rocket science this. Your headline has to be enticing enough to compel users to take their eyes off other interesting stuff on their news feed. The best trick is to tap into the underlying primary motives of your target audience. What is it that stirs your audience emotionally, logically and physically? What makes them sit up, take notice and act? Well yes, the most common and effective primal emotions are lust, greed, fear, sorrow, guilt, and happiness. Channelize these emotions, while also presenting a logical solution. Offer immediate gratification to grab their attention.

How to Create A Blockbuster WordPress Blog in Under 20 Minutes.

Save $12000 Daily on Facebook Fans by Avoiding This Costly Mistake.

Pose question-based headlines while promising to offer a solution.

Tired of Living in Debt? Like Us to Know How to Live a Debt-Free Life!

Do you know the number one emotion that drives people to make purchase related decisions? Fear it is.

Yes, fear is an extremely powerful emotion when it comes to getting people to act upon something. People aren't too open to the prospect of investing in new products because they fear losing money or to make a wrong decision. This is exactly the psychology behind why free products are such a rage when it comes to grabbing the prospective customer's attention.

Free means zero risk, and no risk means zero fear. Headlines offering freebies or free solutions to the user's problems perform brilliantly because there's no risk attached to it.

Keep the copy tight, succinct and engaging (photo ads have a limit of 90 characters). Use clear, straightforward language that's easy to understand. It should trigger your audience's, while also telling them the benefits they can enjoy by liking your or visiting your website. Follow the powerful WIFM (What's In It For Me) principle. Keep it brief with a high lead value.

Facebook has also come up with slideshow ads, where you can create a PowerPoint style slideshow with your best images. Active wear brand Carbon 38 discovered that in comparison to the regular photo ads, slideshow ads offer an 85 percent higher return on your ad spend and a 40 percent increase in click-through rate.

A lot of business and Facebook ventures are converting their most popular content pieces into slideshow ads. You are simply distilling and repackaging your best content into an ad. Think of creative ways to convey the written message into visuals or sum up each point in a few words, and make a killer video ad out of it. Keep the content throughout the video consistent with the final call to action.

Click on the preview option at the bottom of the ad to ensure everything looks good. If you're happy with how the ad looks, tap the "Confirm" button to submit the ad. When the ad is approved by Facebook, you get a notification for the same.

7. Split test multiple ads. Split testing or A/B testing as it's referred to is testing two different ads to conclude which one performs better. It virtually impossible to predict what works and what doesn't even if you know your audience really well. The only way to create profitable ad campaigns is by testing different options to pick out ones that work. You'll know which ads work and which don't when you try various options through split testing.

to make the most of Facebook's split test feature, create different variations of ads that are performing well by altering a single attribute at one time. For instance, pick an ad that's performing well, and create two versions of it by retaining everything else but using two different headlines for both versions.

If you make too many changes in both versions, you won't be able to single out elements that are working well. In the above example, if you were to alter the headline and ad copy, and one ad performs clearly well over the other, you won't know if it was due to the headline or ad copy. Stick to testing a single element at one time.

You can also split test various ad placement options. Have one campaign running for right column ads, another for mobile news feed ads and still another for desktop news feed ads. This strategy allows you to closely monitor your budget than if all options are merged into a single campaign.

8. Use the psychology of visuals and colors to your benefit. Facebook ad pros will share little about the brilliant psychological persuasion powers of specific colors (these are their insider secrets you see). However, I am about to reveal one of the most powerful creative elements of Facebook advertising that almost every successful advertiser is harnessing. The power of visuals and colors. Did you know that 90% of all quick judgments we make related to products/brands are traced back to the most dominant colors in the ad or business logo?

According to a study published in Management Decision, there are some clear scientifically backed trends related to how colors are perceived by different people. While the younger audience prefers bright, flaming shades such as red, orange, and yellow, older folks like cooler colors like green, blue, and purple. With age, people tend to prefer cooler, darker shades.

If you are a fun, peppy youth centric brand, you may want to include bright shades in your Facebook ad. However, keep in mind that just because blue signifies trust, reliability, and dependability, you can't use it if it doesn't fit well with the products you are marketing.

For instance, food product logos and pictures almost always feature bright, flaming colors (red, orange, yellow) that are said to stimulate hunger. Blue is not said to get well with food products as it's associated with poison and chemicals. Find colors that fit your brand's personality, and use them in your ad design, images, and logo. It all boils down to the appropriateness and personal fit. Think about your target audience and use colors that evoke the right psychological triggers in them to expedite their buying decisions.

Chapter Five: 4 Clever Ways to Make Money On Facebook

You know by now that though Facebook is great for sharing pictures of your vacation or establishing connections with old friends, there's a lot of money to be made here by building brands and businesses.

Here are some 10 ingenious ways to turn Facebook into a profit machine.

1. Sell Other People's Products and Services

You've probably heard of affiliate marketing if you have been following the world of internet marketing for a while. It is a fairly profitable business model, where you get a commission for selling other people's products or services.

There are plenty of affiliate marketing marketplaces (such as ClickBank, ShareASale, MaxBounty etc) where you can sign up to promote a variety of products and services. You can also sign up as an affiliate for programs directly through their site if they accept affiliates.

Here are some general guidelines for picking affiliate marketing products on Clickbank

Pick products that have a commission percentage of 50 percent and above except if it's a recurring commission based service/product (in which case you can bring it down to 40 percent). Anything lower than 50-60 percent that is just not worth the time.

Opt for a product with high gravity ratings. These are the products that are performing really well and making affiliate marketers money. However, don't strike off new products with low gravity ratings from your list. They may have a high potential and little competition.

It all boils down to the quality of the sales page and product. If you find a product promising and beneficial for your audience, experiment with it.

When you sign up to be an affiliate or promoter for any product/service, the merchant or marketplace site gives you a unique affiliate link (through which your sales and other stats can be monitored). You include this link in your blog or Facebook posts along with interesting, valuable content. Each time someone makes a purchase by clicking on your unique link, you earn a commission.

Once you've picked your products, build a fan page or community on a topic related to the products/services. For instance, if you are selling a course for copywriters, you may want to create a page or group for copywriting enthusiasts or beginners.

You can offer lots of copywriting tips, content creation ideas etc to win their trust and build authority. Once you've engaged your audience, positioned yourself as an authority and won their trust, it's easy to recommend things to them.

Create a detailed review for the post, and share a link on your fan page or group. Include an impact headline that sums up how the course can help copywriters get started in a profitable industry.

Facebook allows you to share affiliate links as of now as long as it complies with their community standards. Read through their policies first before promoting products and services through affiliate marketing.

There are tons of fan pages dedicated to cars, drones, relationships, homes and just about any topic under the sun. Find a bunch of passionate fans who have a deep interest in the topic, build a strong community around it to gain trust and loyalty, and finally, start promoting high-quality products/services which you think will benefit your audience.

Create a blog around the topic and instead of sending people straight to the buyer page, drive them to your blog post where they can get in-depth information about a topic. The affiliate marketing link can be placed on the blog or at the end of it.

No one like to see tacky looking, long winded links on a Facebook page. Make your links short and professional looking by using a link cloaker software to dress up tawdry affiliate links.

If you are selling more than a single product or service, create separate pages for each program or category of programs. For instance, if you are selling digital products or eBooks related to toddler parenting, create fan page or group for parents of toddlers.

Similarly, cooking related products/services can be combined into a separate group for cooking enthusiasts. This way you are sub-targeting various niches. People don't want to like your page to see a bunch of promotions that they aren't interested in.

You can, of course, repost and share things that are common to groups. For instance, if you come with a post such, "10 Healthy Recipes that Will Get Your toddlers to Lick Their Fingers", it can fit in the cooking as well as parenting page. Do you get the flow?

One of the most important things to keep in mind if you are using affiliate marketing to make money on Facebook is to understand that it is your reputation at stake as an influencer and brand, which means stick to selling only high-quality and valuable products that truly benefit your audience. Don't end up peddling a load of bull or you'll lose these precious audience members and your reputation.

2. Write and Sell eBooks

eBooks are becoming insanely profitable off late owing to the low upfront operational costs involved. There's no cost related to printing and materials since everything is shared electronically. This means anyone with a decent topic or idea can attempt to create an ebook. Plus, it's a nice passive income stream, where you invest some effort to create the book once but reap its benefits forever or each time it's sold.

with its targeted audience and community feel, Facebook has a ready audience for your books if you know how to penetrate the market.

Nonfiction eBooks that offer people how to information or a clear solution to their pressing woes tend to sell well. Currently, the best selling eBooks are books that tell people how to make money with eBooks, which means everyone is interested in savoring a slice of the profitable eBook pie. Unless you have a really gripping tale, a knack for building strong characters, stick to nonfiction.

Start by writing your eBook on a topic or area where you already have some established authority. You don't need shiny credentials to be an eBook author but you should be able to convince people about why they should buy from you over any regular Joe who also writes books. Positioning yourself as an expert will give you an edge when it comes to promoting the book.

Once you've finished drafting your book in a word processor, create a Kindle Direct Publishing account and add your book by following the instructions under Bookshelf < Add New Title.

KDP allows publishers to earn a royalty of 70% if the eBook is priced below $9.99. Keep the price low initially to bag some early bird reviews and ratings, and notch it up once the book gains some traction.

Now comes the fun part. Promoting your book on Facebook. Like all businesses, start by building a community around the topic of your eBook. If it's about flying drones, build a community of people who are passionate about drones.

Here are some smart strategies to promote your eBook on Facebook

Giveaways

No surprise this, people love freebies and giveaways. Distribute a few free copies on the book to loyal and dedicated fans on your page, along with influencers in the niche. Request them to leave behind reviews, and ratings. Kindle Publishing has its own unique algorithms, where if a particular book performs well, Amazon gives it further push by recommending it to customers. If sales soar, it becomes a part of the best selling list.

Consider building an email list through Facebook, where you can communicate with interested readers about updates, news, promotional offers, new launches and informative newsletters.

Also, host sweepstakes and giveaways contests for a copy of the book or other freebies related to the book. Ensure every promotional post has a clear Call to Action, where your audience know exactly what they are supposed to do. Include a mind-blowing eBook cover. Promote the giveaway extensively on your newsletter, blog and social media. Always tag winners in the comments, while also sending them a personal message.

Contests are a great way to get people excited about being a part of your email list. For instance, a pet based business can ask pet owners to send entries for the cutest cat or dog contest. All the photographs can be posted on your Facebook page, and winners can be picked by asking your followers to vote for their favorite picture.

Tabs

Create a separate Tab on your fan page for the book. Let your readers know you as an author and learn more the book. The additional tabs show up right under your Facebook cover image, and can be expanded to offer additional information once users click "More." Visitors can browse through the entire page and explore content that's useful to them. Use this tab feature to your advantage for promoting the book.

Keep your Facebook posts brief and gripping, and add detailed information under specifically created tabs. This way people who want additional information about your products and services can click on relevant tabs for details. Tabs help keep your information distinct and organized. You don't need to cram everything on a single page. Just create a separate tab for each of your books, and make it easy for people to find more information.

Facebook Videos

Apart from using advertising strategies mentioned in the previous chapter to promote your eBooks, readers can also use videos brilliantly to create a buzz about their books. It is such an interesting way to create curiosity about your book, yet marketers fail to cash in on it. Play with 15-second video ads or create interesting video content that piques your audience's curiosity about the book. Don't forget to use the autoplay feature while creating video ads.

You can talk about the highlights of the book in the video. Talk to your customers in an interest grabbing and conversational manner about how they benefit from the book. Introduce a sense of urgency in your voice and tone towards the end of the video when you urge them to take action right away. These videos may give you a better response or conversion rate than direct sales or blatantly promotional runs.

Create Bundle Offers

Creating offers is another cool trick to stay on top of the Facebook eBook marketing/promotional game. You may have more than one book in your eBook portfolio, which means you can bundle them up with smart promotional strategies.

For instance, if customers purchase your first book within the stipulated period, you can offer the next two books for 50 percent off the regular price tag. This will increase the sales of all three books. You can also offer a free copy of the next book.

Offers create a nice buzz for your book on Facebookand help spread a positive word about it. Here's an example – Claim your free copy of my latest book today!

Send the customer to a landing page, where he can claim a copy of your next book by purchasing a copy of your current book.

Focused Groups

Groups offer a precise, targeted and dedicated platform for promoting your eBook. There are literally hundreds of groups/communities on Facebook dedicated to independent authors/publishers, multiple genres, and even well-known authors. Be active in these groups where you can come across several beneficial cross-promotional activities.

It's also a good practice to comment on these groups, engage in group discussions and basically strike a rapport with your target readers.

Keep in mind a few points though before using groups to promote and market your books. First, is your book relevant to the audience of that particular group? If you've created an eBook about taking a luxury cruise holiday, you certainly won't find your audience in a backpacker's group or adventure vacation enthusiasts group.

Find the relevant groups, and increase your conversions by introducing your book to the right audience.

Next, some groups do not take too kindly to overtly promotional posts or promotional links. Always take the time to learn about the group's etiquette and rules before posting or you risk getting banned from the group, thus resulting in an unfavorable reputation. Create your own fan page as an author once you gain considerable popularity.

3. Build an Email List

Building an email list is one of the best ways to establish constant communication with your customers. You can make money by selling physical or digital products on your blog or promote other people's products/services or make money through advertising programs such as Google Adsense if you have a targeted email list of people who are interested in your products or services.

Offer a lead magnet such as a freebie, coupon, eBook, special report etc. much like any opt-in form to entice customers to be a part of your power list. Make it something that's hard to find. Some internet marketing blogs offer their customers a list of the hottest niches for blogs, while others offer free themes, plugins etc. It really depends on exactly what your target audience is after. Give them rare, well-researched and valuable tools, and they'll bite the hook.

Offering exclusive and hard to find content (remember the list of the best performing niches?) in a downloadable format is a great way to offer customers solid value, and get them to return the favor by buying from your or visiting your blog. Not all business deal with physical products, which makes giving away exclusive pieces of content highly lucrative.

Another smart trick you can use is adding a link to your squeeze or lead capture page. Edit your cover image by adding a relevant description for the photo. Include a powerful call to action within the description, followed by a squeeze page link. This will not just give you instant branding on the cover photograph, but also help people reach your opt-in page easily.

You can also include a call to across on your cover photo instead of including it in the description. This way it's prominently displayed across the top of your page as soon as people visit your page, which creates a sense of urgency. You're basically goading people to act fast by including a clear and conspicuous call to action.

Facebook can also be used to retain and build connections with people on your list. When people opt in to your list, send them a welcome email that prompts them to follow you on Facebook and other social media platforms. One of the biggest advantages of this neat tip is even if they unsubscribe from your list in future, they will still receive updates on Facebook and other social media platforms.

Whet your audience's appetite by showing them exactly what they'll get if they sign up for your email list. Share your newsletter on Facebook. The caption should include a link to your opt-in page. What's more? Your Facebook fans will share your newsletter and give you, even more, exposure and subscribers from among their social contacts.

If you are offering a piece of content that's not available anywhere in your upcoming newsletter, use that as bait for signing up people for your email list. This strategy serves a dual purpose. It piques the curiosity of people who aren't on your email list and subsequently gets them to sign up for the list.

Additionally, people who are on your list and haven't been too responsive will also get curious owing to the buzz. They will end up opening a newsletter they wouldn't have bothered about otherwise.

Host Events

Hosting events like an online webinar or creating a real, physical event on Facebook is also a great way of connecting with your target audience, and getting their details. Several internet marketers successfully advertise free webinars using

Facebook's advertising feature. Encourage fans to sign up for a free training or webinar by entering their email.

A free webinar can be advertised like –

Free Training Webinar

Has your online business hit a slump? Looking to shake things up a bit? Instagram could just be what you need to go from average to stupendous.

Join Instagram marketing expert (name) for a stellar, value-packed FREE webinar this Friday at 7:00 pm PST where you can learn some of the fastest ways to skyrocket your business with Instagram. See you there.

Create a post promoting a free webinar and boost the post or send your visitors to a lead opt-in form through Facebook ads.

Why tap online resources? You can also create Facebook events for networking in your city or neighborhood. While registering online for the event, people can be encouraged to opt in to your email list.

4. Sell Physical Products on Facebook

Facebook isn't only about content and connections, there's a whole new market out there for physical products too.

You can create an attractive, comprehensive and targeted virtual storefront on Facebook using an ecommerce platform like Shopify. Many of these ecommerce platforms offer you a free trial to gauge how

The best part about setting up a Facebook store is you can reach a global audience, while constantly engaging with them and growing your business.

How to Create a Facebook Store or Shop Page?

First, log in to your business page. On the timeline just below your page cover photo, there's a section called "Add Shop Section."

Click the blue "Add Shop Section" on the pop-up.

Enter all the required business details.

You need to set-up a payment system next.

The only available payment option on Facebook currently is Stripe, which means you will have to register for a Stripe account if you don't have one already. Set up the payment system.

Once the Stripe account has been set-up, Facebook will redirect you to the main business page. Click on Finish Setup to fill in the remaining details.

You're all set to start selling now!

You should now see a separate "Shop" tab on your business page. Click on the tab and you'll get a box that asks you to add a product to the shop. Click on the "Add Product" link to continue.

Once you click "Add Photos", you can start uploading product images. After uploading images, click on "Use Photos" for your images to go live.

You'll get a "Product Details" field once you've uploaded all images. Write a short, engaging and interesting generating description for each product. Talk about its features and benefits. What sets it apart from other similar products? If there's an existing product description from the original merchant, you can simply seek their permission and copy their product description if it's effectively written.

Once you've uploaded all products, they will be presented in a list style layout, which can be modified. You can view the product image and its price. You also have the option of determining whether you want the product to be available to your fans.

Conclusion

"The secret of getting ahead is getting started."

- *Mark Twain*

Thank you for downloading *Facebook Marketing: A Comprehensive Guide for Building Authority, Creating Engagement and Making Money through Facebook.*

I genuinely hope this book was able to offer you lots of little tips, proven strategies and wisdom nuggets for building a powerful and profitable Facebook business.

I've tried to keep the techniques as straightforward and actionable as possible so even beginners can get their feet wet in the lucrative world of Facebook marketing.

The next step is to start applying these valuable tips immediately. Pick tips that work for you and work towards building a loyal community of buyers. At the end of the day, social media marketing is all about creating engagement, strengthening credibility, building strong brands, and eventually setting up a community of loyal buyers who turn out to be your most powerful evangelists.

Try different strategies and techniques, and pick the one that offers you the best results. You'll learn a lot of things along the course of your journey.

Lastly, if you enjoyed reading the book, please take the time to share your thoughts by posting a review on Amazon. It'd be highly appreciated...

Check Out My Other Books

Below you'll find some of my other popular books that are popular on Amazon and Kindle as well. Simply click on the links below to check them out. Alternatively, you can visit my <u>author page</u> on Amazon to see other work done by me.

https://www.amazon.com/Mark-Smith/e/B01JZ91Q5E/ref=ntt_dp_epwbk_0

www.ingramcontent.com/pod-product-compliance
Lightning Source LLC
Chambersburg PA
CBHW071515210326
41597CB00018B/2765